Next Level Recruiting

9 Stages of the Talent Acquisition Life Cycle

Kelly Robinson

ABSOLUTE AUTHOR PUBLISHING HOUSE

NEXT LEVEL RECRUITING
Copyright © 2020 by Kelly Robinson
All Rights Reserved.

Publisher: Absolute Author Publishing House
Editor: Dr. Melissa Caudle
Formatter: Anni And Clara
Cover Design: Rebecacovers
Cover Photo: Sean Morse Photography

LIBRARY OF CONGRESS CATALOGUE IN-PUBLICATION-DATA

Paperback ISBN: 978-1-64953-050-9
eBook ISBN: 979-8-89401-064-9

p. cm.

1. Business. 2. Hiring Advice. 3. Career

For Erik, because everything is for you.
Love you more, Mommy.

NEXT LEVEL RECRUITING

TABLE OF CONTENTS

NEXT LEVEL RECRUITING

What Does Panna Know?

Hey there! I'm Kelly Robinson, Founder and CEO of Panna Knows Recruiting (PKR). If you're curious about what makes this book worth your time, let's start with obvious questions I get all the time: **What's with the name?** Why Panna Knows? Who—or what—is Panna? People are always curious, and that's exactly why I didn't call it "Kelly Robinson Coaching LLC" or "Kelly Robinson Recruiting, Inc." (Yawn, right?) I wanted something different. Something that sparks conversations. And here we are!

So, what does Panna mean?

Panna comes from *Pali*, a Sanskrit language, and it translates to **wisdom.**

Here's the fun part—when I told my then nine-year-old son Erik, he laughed and said, "Oh, so you're ancient!" (Cue my dramatic gasp.) That moment made me realize how often we equate wisdom with age, but true wisdom is about learning through experience—navigating challenges, making mistakes, and growing from them. It's about what you do with what you've learned, and that's a lesson I strive to carry forward in every aspect of my work. I had to explain that wisdom isn't just about age. It's about **learning through experience**—those lessons that come from navigating challenges, making mistakes, and figuring things out as you go. Sure, I've spent over 20 years in recruiting (so yeah, not exactly a rookie), but wisdom doesn't have to take decades to develop. It's about **applying what you've learned** to create positive change—for yourself and for others. At PKR, wisdom drives everything we do. It's about turning insights into impact and helping companies and candidates make connections that truly work.

Why should you care?

Because recruiting is a dirty word, yep, I said it. Ask anyone—candidates, hiring managers, recruiters themselves—and they'll tell you how frustrating the process can be. But here's the thing: it doesn't have to be that way.

We need to stop screening people in or out based on surface-level impressions and start focusing on what really matters—**building relationships, listening, and making genuine connections.** Unlike traditional recruiting methods that often rely on rigid checklists or arbitrary filters, this approach emphasizes understanding the full picture—what makes a candidate tick, what the hiring manager truly needs, and how to bridge those gaps for a lasting, meaningful fit. Great recruiting is about more than filling a role. It's about creating strong matches that work for everyone involved. At PKR, we approach every search with the mindset of a true partnership, aligning the goals of hiring managers and candidates to build something lasting.

So, what does Panna know?

Panna Knows is built around a framework of **9 stages of recruiting**, broken into digestible pieces that ensure consistency and excellence in every search. These stages cover everything from defining the perfect candidate profile to crafting a compelling offer and ensuring post-hire success. They're designed to guide you through a framework that you can customize for your own needs, making recruiting intentional, thoughtful, and effective. I am not here to train you in the basics of recruiting. I am here to show you the value that you can provide for candidates and hiring managers beyond fillings seats. Why 9 stages? Because recruiting isn't something you should wing. Each stage matters. Each stage ensures you're doing right by your company, candidates, and yourself.

The 9 stages reflect the lessons I've learned about the importance of communication in recruiting over decades of experience, from defining the perfect candidate profile to ensure post-hire success. It's a roadmap to doing recruitment intentionally, thoughtfully, and effectively. And consistency? It's the secret sauce. Whether it's your first hire or your hundredth, the process works when you follow it every time.

This book isn't about learning how to recruit. It's about the importance of collaboration, relationships, transparency, and integrity in everything you do.

Why this book?

This isn't just another recruiting book filled with fluff. It's a practical guide packed with actionable insights to fix what's broken in the recruiting process and create real, lasting connections. It's about creating intentionality in your recruiting process, listening to what your candidates and hiring managers need, and building a system that leads to long-term success.

What makes this book different? It's actionable. It's built on real-world experience, tested framework, and the wisdom of knowing what works (and what doesn't). If you're tired of the same old, same old in recruiting and want to learn how to make genuine connections and lasting matches, this book is for you. And hey, who knows? You might even gain a little "panna" of your own along the way.

I am not here to teach you how to recruit, I am here to show you how to take your recruiting to the next level using my framework and philosophy on communication.

Let's dive in and get recruiting right one stage at a time.

Stage 1 - Defining Requirements

Imagine sitting down with a hiring manager who just had their top performer leave the team. The stakes are high, and they expect even higher. When recruiters first connect with a hiring manager about a position, it's crucial to dig deep and truly understand the needs. This is where the foundation of a successful hire begins. There are three key areas to cover during this intake process, and while it might take 30–45 minutes, that investment of time upfront will save you exponentially in the long run.

Here's what you need to uncover:

1. **The Drive for the Need**
2. **The Profile**
3. **The Culture**

Each of these elements is essential to understanding the role, the team, and how to make the right match. Let's dive into each one.

1. The Drive for the Need - Why is this position open?

Understanding the "why" behind the position is critical. Is this a newly created role? Is it open due to growth, restructuring, or turnover? Each scenario provides a valuable context:

- **Growth**: That's exciting! Dive into the company's growth history and future vision to better position the role of candidates.
- **Restructuring**: Find out what's driving the new products, delivery challenges, or strategic shifts?
- **Turnover**: Was the departure voluntary or involuntary? Was the previous employee a fit for the role, team, or company culture? Understanding these dynamics will help you tailor your search and address candidate concerns.

Don't shy away from addressing negatives. For example, if the company has poor Glassdoor reviews, be upfront about what they're doing to improve. I've seen firsthand how being transparent about challenges, paired with specific examples of how the company is addressing them, can transform candidate perceptions. For instance, one company openly acknowledged their low employee engagement scores but highlighted their new leadership training program and quarterly feedback sessions as steps toward improvement. This approach-built trust and helped attract candidates who wanted to be part of the solution. Candidates value transparency, and addressing potential concerns head-on will build trust.

By understanding the "drive," you'll not only gain clarity on the role, but also equip yourself to answer smart candidates' questions and ensure a stronger match.

2. The Profile - What will this person do, and what are they bringing to the table?

Go beyond a list of top skills and dig into the day-to-day responsibilities and attributes needed for success in the role. Here are some key questions to guide your conversation:

- What attributes are critical for success in this role?
- What does a productive day look like?
- Who will this person interact with daily?
- How does this role impact department and company objectives?
- Where does the ideal candidate come from (industry, company size, etc.)?
- What opportunities for growth does this role offer within the company?

Understanding the full picture helps you identify candidates who align not just with the role, but with the team's objectives. For example, if a team's primary objective is to improve cross-department collaboration, you might prioritize candidates with persuasive communication, collaboration, and relationship-building skills. By matching these qualities with the team's goals, you create a synergy that ensures long-term success. Remember, hiring managers will appreciate the extra effort, and it will set you apart as a recruiter who truly understands their needs.

3. The Culture - What is the department culture like?

Company culture is important, but department culture can vary significantly and is often the key to finding the right fit. Here are some areas to explore:

- Who makes up the team, and what are their roles?
- What are their backgrounds and experiences?
- What works well in this department, and what doesn't?
- Who are the top performers, and why?
- What hasn't worked in the past?

Understanding the nuances of department culture will help you find candidates who not only have the right skills but also seamlessly fit into the team dynamic. For example, a department that thrives on collaboration may not be the best fit for someone who prefers independent work—and vice versa.

Departments often have unique habits and workflows that differ from the broader company culture. It's also worth noting these nuances early on to understand how the department operates day-to-day. Maybe the team works remotely more often, skips happy hours, or collaborates primarily via email. These details matter when making a successful match.

Final Thoughts

Defining requirements is about more than just checking boxes. Of course you'll cover all the basics of compensation, benefits, etc. in addition to these areas. This book isn't about the basics, it's about the authenticity in recruiting, in relating to people, in doing the right thing. It's about digging deep to understand the role, the team, and the bigger picture. Take the time to ask the right questions, uncover the details, and lay the groundwork for success. By doing so, you're not just filling a position, you're building a foundation for long-term growth and thriving teams. When you take the time upfront to ask the right questions, you set yourself—and your hiring manager—up for success.

After all, our ultimate goal is to hire for retention and long-term success, ensuring both the candidate and the department thrive.

Stage 2 - Building a Sourcing Strategy

Sourcing strategies are the backbone of effective recruiting. They ensure you're not just casting a wide net but casting it in the right waters. Now that we've taken a deep dive into the first stage, Defining Requirements, and laid the groundwork for understanding the need, the profile, and the department culture, it's time to move on to the very crucial—and often overlooked—second stage.

Building a Sourcing Strategy

I can already imagine the collective eye roll I am getting right now. I get it; your instinct is to dive right into the hunt. You've got your keywords, a list of target companies, and LinkedIn fired up. But let me emphasize why crafting a sourcing strategy—and more importantly, tracking is fundamental to your efficiency. (Trust me, it can even be fun!)

Proactive and Reactive Sourcing

A robust sourcing strategy encompasses both proactive (hunting) and reactive (posting) efforts. Hunting involves actively searching for candidates through tools like LinkedIn, networking events, and direct outreach, while posting focuses on attracting candidates by creating compelling job ads and sharing them on platforms like job boards and social media. Engaging both active and passive candidates ensures you have a strong, diverse pipeline. Leverage your Applicant Tracking System (ATS), Talent Intelligence Platform, social media, standard job boards, employee referrals, Google searches, and other niche resources to cast a wide net.

Efficiency Through Tracking

About that tracking, there is no need to overcomplicate it! A simple spreadsheet can work wonders. Record your keywords, search strings, and sources, noting what works and what doesn't. The goal is to take a data-driven approach that enables you to evaluate, refine, and adapt your strategy.

Cross-Referencing and Validation

Keywords and job titles are just the starting point. Keep in mind that different companies may use various titles for similar roles. For instance, a "Software Engineer" at one company might be called a "Developer" or "Software Developer" at another. Recognizing these variations can help you expand your search and identify qualified candidates more effectively. Cross-reference and track these nuances. For example, if a developer with the required skills is commanding a $20,000 higher salary at one company, that's critical intel for your search—and for setting expectations with hiring managers. Document these findings and cross-reference them with companies, job titles, skill sets, and sourcing sites to stay ahead of the game.

Test, Refine, Repeat

Your sourcing strategy is a living, breathing process. Test it, refine it based on your findings, and use what you learn to build a solid foundation. Tracking not only makes you more efficient but also helps you quickly find the right candidates when similar searches arise in the future.

Diversify Your Avenues

Don't rely solely on LinkedIn. Dig into your database, tap into your network, and share job postings widely. For example, platforms like Meetup or industry-specific forums can be goldmines for niche talent, providing access to candidates who might not be actively searching but are highly engaged in their field. Explore less conventional avenues—they might surprise you. For specific roles, social media platforms can yield great results. Join groups, read discussions, engage, and ask other recruiters where they search. The internet is your treasure trove—use it.

Empathy in Strategy Building

Put yourself in the candidate's shoes. Ask yourself, "Where do these candidates spend their time? What do they like to do? Where do they hang out online?" For example, I once sourced candidates for a creative design role and discovered many of them were active in niche forums like Dribbble and Behance. By tailoring my outreach to these platforms and engaging with their portfolios, I was able to connect with highly qualified and passionate candidates. Understanding their digital habits enhances your outreach and increases your credibility. Tailor your strategy to meet them where they are. Understanding their digital habits enhances your outreach and increases your credibility.

Job Boards and Credibility

Yes, job boards can be valuable, especially for specific types of roles. Remember, the effectiveness of job boards is always evolving. Don't be afraid to revisit avenues that didn't work in the past—they might yield results this time around. Knowing which tools work for which types of searches demonstrate your expertise and builds trust with hiring managers.

Final Thoughts

Here's to a strategic and efficient sourcing journey—one backed by reasons, data, and results. And if you hit a snag, don't hesitate to reach out for help.

Happy hunting!

Stage 3 - Reviewing the Resume

So far, we've defined the requirements and built a sourcing strategy. Now, we move to Stage 3 of the Talent Acquisition Life Cycle: reviewing the resume.

This stage involves evaluating a candidate's resume at three distinct points in the recruitment process:

1. **Prior to reaching out**
2. **Prior to a phone interview**
3. **During the phone interview**

(Yes, I like the number three. Most things in recruiting can be broken down into threes. So, expect more of those to come!)

1. Prior to Reaching Out

Your first encounter with a resume often happens online—whether on a Talent Intelligence Platform,

ATS, on job boards, or through referrals. Each platform has its nuances: Talent Intelligence Platforms offer advanced analytics and AI-driven insights, helping to identify patterns and potential matches that might otherwise be overlooked; ATS systems often display standardized formatting but can miss key details; job boards may provide a mix of polished and underdeveloped resumes; referrals often come with informal context that may require follow-up for clarity. Understanding these differences helps you approach resumes with the right mindset. Keep in mind that not all resumes are crafted the way you might prefer, and LinkedIn profiles are not resumes.

Be open-minded! Don't judge solely based on a profile or resume. LinkedIn serves as a platform to highlight skills and abilities but doesn't necessarily offer a comprehensive work history. Cross-reference the information you find on LinkedIn but always request a comprehensive resume from the candidate during your initial contact. For example, LinkedIn might show an impressive list of skills but omit key details like project specifics or achievements. I once encountered a candidate whose LinkedIn profile highlighted their software engineering background but completely omitted their leadership role in a major product launch—critical information that was only revealed through their full resume. This ensures you're working with complete and accurate information.

2. Prior to a Phone Interview

Preparation is key! Reviewing the resume before a phone or video interview sets you up for a more informed and productive conversation.

If needed, request the candidate's resume within 24-48 hours of your initial outreach, either through email or your ATS messaging system. This provides ample time for review and preparation. A thorough review allows you to:

- Understand their career progression.
- Identify and clarify any gaps.

Align their experience with the position you're recruiting for. This step is crucial for ensuring that you approach the interview with the right context and questions, demonstrating your professionalism and understanding.

3. During the Phone Interview

This is where you dive deeper! A resume is just the starting point; your goal is to fill in the gaps and truly understand the candidate's story.

Focus on the last 5–7 years of their career (or their last three roles unless the search requires further exploration). This approach is particularly valuable in fast-moving industries like tech or finance, where recent experience often reflects the most relevant skills and tools. For other roles, such as those in leadership or academia, earlier experiences might also hold significant weight, so tailor your focus accordingly. Ask questions to uncover details such as:

- How they found it.
- Why they accepted it.
- What they achieved in the role.
- What they wish could have changed if given the opportunity. (People, process, tools, comp, location, etc.)
- Why they left.

Understanding these motivations helps you make informed decisions and align candidates with opportunities that truly fit their goals and aspirations.

Why it Matters?

Your reputation as a recruiter is closely tied to the quality of the matches you make. Quality can be demonstrated through measurable outcomes like high retention rates, positive feedback from hiring managers, and candidates thriving in their roles. Showcasing these successes in reviews or during discussions with hiring teams helps reinforce your value and credibility. It's not just about having a bubbly personality or being likable, it's about delivering quality and success. Hiring managers value recruiters who consistently connect them with candidates that contribute to retention and long-term success. Strive for excellence in every match.

Key Takeaways

Don't solely rely on LinkedIn profiles; always request a comprehensive resume.

Prepare for phone interviews by thoroughly reviewing resumes in advance.

During phone interviews, investigate the last few positions or the last 5–7 years of their career, focusing on motivations behind job changes. Past events and actions often predict future events and actions.

Focus on quality matches, not quantity—screen OUT candidates who aren't the best fit.

Prioritize making solid matches that contribute to retention and success for both employers and candidates.

Remember, reviewing resumes isn't just about checking boxes; it's about uncovering the story behind the career path. By doing so, you elevate your credibility and ensure long-term success for both candidates and your company.

Final Thoughts

Reviewing resumes is more than a step in the process, it's art and science. It requires curiosity, attention to detail, and a commitment to uncovering the story behind each candidate's career journey. By taking the time to evaluate resumes thoughtfully, you not only build trust with hiring managers, but also set the stage for successful, long-term hires. Remember, the goal is to make quality matches that benefit both the candidate and the employer. When you master this stage, you solidify your reputation as a recruiter who delivers excellence every time.

Stage 4 - Prequalification

We have covered a ton thus far. Let's review the stages we covered:

- ✓ Stage 1: Defining the Requirements
- ✓ Stage 2: Building a Sourcing Strategy
- ✓ Stage 3: Reviewing the Resume

And now, we are on Stage 4 of the Talent Acquisition Life Cycle: Prequalification.

In this stage, we take a deep dive into three critical areas with a candidate:

1. **Skill Set**
2. **Attributes**
3. **Fit – Department and Company**

The Prequalification process is only as good as the work you have done in Stages 1, 2, and 3. Stage 1 ensures you understand the role and its requirements, Stage 2 provides a clear and effective sourcing strategy, and Stage 3 focuses on reviewing resumes thoroughly to identify the best potential matches. Together, these stages lay the groundwork for success in pre-qualifying candidates effectively. If you have a hard time at this point, you have to go back and analyze the work you've done thus far and make a change. This is where the sourcing strategy tracking is really key! It's always best to do that right away instead of waiting. The hiring manager will truly appreciate the market intelligence and information you can share with them instead of wasting time.

While it all feels like a lot of work to get to this point, it will save you time in the long run. You will hire more quickly than if you wing it. I promise. Here are the three critical areas of pre-qualification:

1. Skill Set

Understanding the top three or four skill sets or competencies is vital on the initial call with your hiring manager. Even if you, as a recruiter, may not have the technical skills, drilling into these competencies helps in pre-qualifying candidates.

It is crucial to ensure that candidates have the necessary skills to perform the job successfully.

Ask the hiring managers a few questions to better understand if the candidate is qualified to move to the next step. For example, hiring managers might ask about a candidate's experience with specific tools, how they have overseen past challenges relevant to the role, or their approach to teamwork and collaboration.

These tailored questions can help you evaluate the candidate's alignment with the role more effectively.

2. Attributes

Attributes or personal characteristics are unique to each individual. Recognizing what attributes the hiring manager values in a potential employee is crucial. Whether it's problem-solving skills, passion, or a drive to make an impact, understanding these attributes helps in screening candidates effectively during the call.

3. Fit – Department and Company

Departmental Fit: Understanding the culture of the department is essential.

Company Fit: Assessing the overall fit involves aligning with the company's culture, environment, goals, and objectives. Ensuring candidates are in sync with these aspects is crucial for a successful long-term match.

Questions to consider include:

- What are the objectives?
- What is collaboration/interaction like?
- What is the communication style?
- What are the remote work options?
- What is the mission?
- What are the values?
- What are the goals?

All of these can be answered for the role, the

department, and the business. Understanding these and then being able to extract information to validate or uncover if a candidate is a fit is critical. It takes practice, sheer interest in making a really strong match, screening OUT and not in.

Prescreening

- Create a standard questionnaire you can use with the basic recruitment questions like:
- Why are you looking?
- Are you currently working (always qualify, don't assume)?
- What changes would you make to your current/last role if you were able to? (this helps you to understand them psychologically a bit more, and you may be able to qualify them solely on this question).
- What is your total comp goal (get details on base, bonus, commission, 401k, shares, benefits, PTO, WFH, etc.)?
- What is the most important part of the comp package to you and why?

- When can you start a new role?
- When can you interview?

Take your basic questions and create a template. You can add specific questions for each search to evaluate skill sets, attributes, and culture. We review this as part of my training/coaching.

Assessments

Utilizing assessments to evaluate a candidate's skills, attributes, and overall fit can be beneficial. It provides a more structured and objective approach to screening, ensuring that the right candidates progress in the recruitment process. My philosophy is that assessments should be used as only part of the process. Decisions should not be made on them alone. These can be done in various stages of the process as well.

Presenting Candidates

Once a candidate aligns with the required skill set, attributes, and cultural fit—and the basics (these are important; don't skip them or assume anything)—it's time to present them to the hiring manager.

This is not a time to sell; it's a time to be clear on what the candidate brings to the table and what they may be lacking. If they lack one of the fundamental skills or are asking for compensation way over the target, you would not present these candidates (and hopefully, you didn't spend more time than necessary on them). However, you can and should share this data with your hiring manager. It helps them to understand what you are learning in the market and better evaluate the candidates you are sending to them.

Ensure all decision-makers are available for evaluation when moving to the interview. You do not want to create an unpleasant experience for the candidate. You also don't want to cut corners. Know in advance what the process will be and make sure your candidate and the hiring team are all on board and that they make the time. The goal is to screen OUT candidates who are not the right fit.

Final Thoughts

Prequalification is where the foundation you've built in earlier stages truly comes to life. This stage is not about rushing, it's about understanding and aligning candidates with the needs of the role, the department, and the company. When done well, prequalification saves time, builds trust, and ensures stronger, longer-lasting matches. Remember, your goal is to create value for both the candidate and the employer, and that starts with a thorough and thoughtful prequalification process. You've got this!

Stage 5 - Interviewing

We've tackled:

- ✓ Stage 1: Defining the Requirements and the three critical areas to uncover.
- ✓ Stage 2: Building Sourcing Strategy and why we need to track and test our work and use various avenues to uncover top talent.
- ✓ Stage 3: Resume Review and the three crucial times to do this.
- ✓ Stage 4: Prequalification and the three areas to cover there: Skill Set, Attributes, Fit.
- ✓ Now onto Stage 5: Interviewing.

Regardless of your role as an interviewer, the objectives remain consistent: ensuring candidates possess the required skills, attributes, and overall fit for the department and company.

There are three things to keep in mind during the

interview process:

1. **Preparation is Key / Structured Approach**
2. **Consistency in Questions**
3. **Creating a Comfortable Environment**

Let's never forget that creating a positive candidate experience is important at every step, but a face-to-face meeting, whether in the office or on a video, is crucial as a first impression. To set up a successful meeting, ensure you have a quiet, professional setting with minimal distractions, and prepare relevant questions in advance. For virtual interviews, test your technology, including camera, microphone, and internet connection, to avoid technical issues. These small steps create a seamless experience, allowing candidates to showcase their personality and communication style while giving hiring teams a chance to assess soft skills and cultural fit in real-time. For example, a candidate's ability to maintain composure and enthusiasm during a video call could indicate their readiness to work effectively in a remote environment. Additionally, hiring managers should review the candidate's profile and prior stages of the process to tailor questions and set the right tone for the discussion. (Yes, the recruiters also contributed greatly during the previous stages, but we are now on the interviewer's part.)

1. Preparation is Key / Structured Approach

As a hiring manager, ensure thorough preparation for the interview. Nothing can be more detrimental than an unprepared interviewer. Know who is responsible for covering each aspect, skills, attributes, and overall fit. Lack of preparation can adversely impact the candidate's experience and the effectiveness of the interview process.

Even in a less formal setting, maintain a structured interview approach. A structured approach benefits both the interviewer and the candidate by providing a clear roadmap for the conversation, ensuring no critical aspects are overlooked. For example, starting with an introduction to set expectations, followed by skill and competency questions, and concluding with time for the candidate's questions can create a balanced and efficient dialogue. This structure keeps the process focused while giving candidates a fair opportunity to present themselves.

For example, you could use a standard format that includes an introduction, questions covering skills and attributes, situational problem-solving scenarios, and time for the candidate to ask questions. This ensures that all critical aspects are addressed while leaving room for a natural flow of conversation. Cover the necessary areas—skills, attributes, and overall fit—while allowing for a natural flow of conversation. A structured yet flexible approach ensures that critical aspects are evaluated without overwhelming the candidate.

2. Consistency in Questions

It's entirely acceptable to ask the same questions during the interview as was discussed in the prequalification call with the recruiter. Leaving something unresolved in your mind or unanswered because you are concerned about repeating questions to dig in deeper can do more harm in the long run than reviewing the question again. This consistency helps in evaluating how candidates express themselves directly and provides an opportunity to hear their responses firsthand.

- Have they been consistent in their answers?
- Did we miss anything?
- Were they able to clarify a question fully?

3. Creating a Comfortable Environment

Consider steering away from panel interviews. While panel interviews can sometimes provide diverse perspectives and offer hiring managers, the chance to see how candidates respond under scrutiny they may also overwhelm candidates, preventing them from presenting their best selves. For example, in situations requiring collaboration across departments, or at the executive and leadership levels, a panel might be useful to evaluate how candidates engage with diverse teams. However, for deeper, more focused conversations, a one-on-one approach often allows candidates to express their experiences more authentically, reflecting how they would behave in day-to-day work scenarios. A one-on-one interview often allows candidates to feel comfortable elaborating on their experiences, leading to a more accurate assessment of their skills and fit.

Create an environment where candidates feel at ease. The goal is to display their true selves. The traditional tactic of creating high-pressure situations during interviews might lead to hiring candidates who excel under pressure or in interviews but struggle in real job scenarios. A more comfortable interview environment is likely to yield a better reflection of the candidate's capabilities and their true self.

Candidate Experience

The interview process is not just an evaluation for the candidate, but also an opportunity for you to showcase your company. Avoid selling your business the entire time. Strike a balance by highlighting your company's strengths and values while focusing on the candidate's fit for the role. Share relevant details about your organization that align with the candidate's interests or career goals, but leave ample space for evaluating their qualifications and discussing how they would contribute to the team. This is not only about you. It needs to be a good fit all around. Offering an outstanding experience reflects positively on your organization and can impact the candidate's decision-making process. Following these three steps for interviews is key to the experience you are creating. Remember, it's not just about finding the right candidate for today; it's about finding the right fit for the long term.

Final Thoughts

Interviewing is where all the preparation and groundwork come together. For example, the clarity achieved during Stage 1, when defining role requirements helps ensure that the right questions are asked, and the thorough sourcing from Stage 2 guarantees a pool of candidates who align with the job profile. Each stage builds upon the other, culminating in a structured, meaningful interview that sets the stage for finding the best fit. It's the moment to engage candidates, evaluate their potential, and create a lasting impression of your company. By focusing on preparation, consistency, and a candidate-friendly environment, you can ensure meaningful and productive interviews. Remember, interviews aren't just about filling a role; they're about building lasting relationships and setting the stage for long-term success.

Stage 6 - Decisioning

In Stage 6 of the Talent Acquisition Life Cycle, the focus is on Decision-making, a crucial step in ensuring the right fit between the candidate and the position.

By this time, you already know all the stages and have hopefully put them to use as you read them. Here's a quick recap:

- ✓ Stage 1 - Defining Requirements ensures you have a clear understanding of the role.
- ✓ Stage 2 - Building Sourcing Strategies focuses on creating and testing ways to find top talent.
- ✓ Stage 3 - Resume Review identifies strong candidates by evaluating their backgrounds thoroughly.
- ✓ Stage 4 - Prequalification hones in on skill sets, attributes, and fit; and
- ✓ Stage 5 - Interviews provide deeper insights

into the candidate's qualifications. Now, we move on to Stage 6: Decision-making!

Here are three ways to arrive at a decision with your hiring managers:

1. **Clearly Defined Evaluation Criteria**
2. **Debrief Sessions**
3. **Drive to Answer**

Recruiters play a crucial role in facilitating the decision-making process. They act as a bridge between candidates and hiring managers, ensuring that feedback is effectively communicated. They also use their expertise to gauge not just the technical fit but also the cultural alignment. Don't leave them out of this process.

Let's drive to a decision and get to the offer, shall we?

1. Clearly Defined Evaluation Criteria

When partnering with the hiring team on decision-making, interviews with candidates should have started in Stage 1 with skills, attributes, and overall fit clearly defined.

If these criteria were appropriately described, you should be at the point of meeting no more than three candidates. Limiting the pool to three ensures a manageable and focused evaluation process, enabling hiring managers to make informed decisions without feeling overwhelmed. It also allows for meaningful comparisons while maintaining efficiency and a positive candidate experience. The best practice is to maintain a ratio of 3:1, candidate interviews to offer.

If you find that your hiring managers need to interview more than three candidates or are declining your candidates, consider revisiting Stage 1 to redefine requirements. Once you do, adjust your sourcing strategy and prescreening questions accordingly.

The need to interview more than three candidates can happen when there is a new hiring manager, a manager new to hiring, or a newly created role. Be patient and consider these needs upfront when advising and working with the hiring manager. Sometimes, they are learning along the way with us. Guide them by providing market intelligence and any information you gather along the way about the market and their specific hiring needs.

2. Debrief Sessions

At the same time a candidate is interviewed, the recruiter should schedule a debrief session with the candidate and with the interview team. Debrief sessions should be scheduled within 24-72 hours of the interview to ensure timely feedback and maintain momentum in the hiring process. This timeframe keeps impressions fresh, allowing for more accurate assessments and enabling swift next steps for both candidates and hiring teams. This allows for timely feedback and ensures that impressions are fresh in everyone's minds.

Note to hiring team: Make time to provide prompt feedback to the recruiter and incorporate them in the feedback loop; it fosters a sense of true partnership and motivates all parties involved. This feedback is valuable for recruiters to understand the hiring manager's perspective and make informed decisions about the next steps. It creates efficiency in the process and helps the recruiter respond in a timely manner to candidates with clear and concise feedback when appropriate.

3. Drive to Answer

It's very important to focus on how the candidate qualifies or doesn't qualify against the role—not necessarily against other candidates. Comparing candidates to each other can divert focus from the actual role. Instead, focus on the role; if you end up with competing candidates, compare them only to determine the best fit.

If a hiring manager ends an interview and can't decide on a candidate, either 1) they didn't get enough information from the candidate to make a decision, or 2) the candidate is more than likely not a fit, but the hiring manager feels like they are "close enough" or "haven't seen enough candidates" and they want the recruiter to "keep them warm."

It's the position of the recruiter to push back on this. Candidates who are kept warm are rarely hired, and if they are, it often isn't a long-term fit. Encourage the hiring manager not to put people "on hold" or "keep them warm." It creates a poor candidate experience and becomes a waste of the recruiter's time keeping them updated every three to four days, knowing the candidate isn't going to be hired.

This is a great time for the recruiter to go back to the qualifications with the hiring manager and review the candidate against the role. The recruiter can help craft questions the hiring manager needs to ask to get to a decision or even do additional digging themselves.

Gut Instincts

It is a controversial topic, but I strongly believe that trusting one's gut instincts is an integral part of decision-making. If something feels off or there's a misalignment between what a candidate is saying and what is observed, these gut feelings should be considered. Sometimes, gut instincts provide insights that go beyond tangible criteria.

Gut feelings are usually directly correlated with past experiences. For instance, I once worked with a candidate whose resume and responses aligned perfectly with the role's requirements, but something about their demeanor during the interview raised concerns. Trusting my gut, I probed further, discovering inconsistencies in their claims about past projects. This deeper dive confirmed my instinct and saved the company from a potential mismatch. These areas certainly deserve some more digging to be validated. But be sure you are not researching any aspects that don't specifically correlate to this role.

Final Thoughts

The decision-making stage is not just about choosing a candidate; it's about selecting the right candidate for the long-term success of both the individual and the organization. For example, I once placed a candidate who wasn't the most technically skilled in the pool but had exceptional alignment with the company's values and goals. This individual not only excelled in the role but also became a key contributor to the company's culture and led a major project that drove significant revenue growth. The right fit can create a ripple effect of success for everyone involved. Trust the process, leverage timely feedback, and keep refining the approach for continuous improvement. Before reaching the offer stage, ensure that the candidate has been fully qualified based on skills, attributes, and overall fit. Decision-making requires a balance of structured criteria, timely communication, and a touch of gut instinct.

The interview serves as a tool to qualify the candidate for the role, but the actual ability to perform on the job is yet to be seen. Pre-closing discussions conducted by the recruiter should cover aspects such as compensation, start date, notice period, and other relevant details.

Let's move on to the next and make an offer!

Stage 7 - Making an Offer

In Stage 7 of the Talent Acquisition Life Cycle, the focus shifts to making a job offer to the selected candidate.

Now we get to the good stuff. I could write a book solely on pre-closing and offers. Here are three things to work through prior to the offer:

1. **Who will make the offer?**
2. **What are the next steps?**
3. **Set Expectations at each contact point.**

It's so critical at this stage that the recruiter is fully aware of what their candidate wants, will consider taking, will absolutely take, and what they will not consider. If you got this far and still don't have a clear understanding of your candidate's expectations, it's worth revisiting Stages 1–6 to ensure you've covered all the groundwork. Thorough preparation at earlier stages is key to maintaining your professional reputation and avoiding unnecessary guesswork. Take the guessing out of the equation by doing the work.

1. Who will make the offer?

Having built a relationship with the candidate and having pre-closed on various aspects, the recruiter usually makes a verbal offer. This is a critical step as recruiters are well-versed in the candidate's expectations and can handle negotiations effectively.

While there may be instances where the hiring manager wants to be directly involved in making the offer to convey passion and excitement about the company, it's suggested that the recruiter make the verbal offer. Recruiters are better positioned and experienced to navigate job negotiations and have a more intimate understanding of the candidate's expectations. For example, I once worked with a candidate who had concerns about their relocation package. By proactively addressing this during preclosure conversations, I was able to craft a tailored offer that not only met their needs but also avoided lengthy negotiations, ensuring a smooth and positive experience for both parties.

Allowing the hiring manager to make the offer directly might bring some risks. Upon hearing the hiring manager's excitement, candidates might attempt to renegotiate the offer, potentially leading to complications. To avoid this, the recruiter, who has established a relationship with the candidate and has pre-closed and gained the candidate's commitment, should handle the verbal offer.

2. What are the next steps?

Human Resources should be sending out the offer letter and starting any necessary background checks, reference checks, etc. (Yes, reference checks can be valuable if you do them right, but no one does them right, so don't waste time unless you've trained with me.)

After the verbal offer is made, the hiring manager should follow up with the candidate to express excitement and welcome them aboard. This can be done through a phone call followed by an email. This follow-up action demonstrates genuine enthusiasm for the candidate joining the team, strengthening their perception of the company as attentive and professional. It also reassures the candidate about their decision, making them feel valued and confident in their choice.

By entrusting the recruiter with the verbal offer, organizations can leverage the built rapport and understanding of the candidate's expectations, leading to smoother negotiations and a positive candidate experience. In addition, it sends the message to the candidate that the recruiter is highly valued as part of the decision-making process. The hiring manager's involvement in the follow-up reinforces the enthusiasm and sets a positive tone for the candidate's onboarding journey.

3. Set Expectations

Timely communication is crucial throughout the offer stage. The recruiter and hiring manager should coordinate closely to ensure that all aspects of the offer are well-communicated and that any questions or concerns from the candidate are addressed promptly.

They should also be in close contact with Human Resources to understand where the new hire is in the process and gain insight into the training and onboarding. The recruiter can keep the candidate close and update them often.

The recruiter should be aware of the candidate's resignation and timeline. Coach them through this! I am a huge proponent of this. Provide guidance on crafting a professional resignation letter, navigating difficult conversations with their current employer, and managing their notice period effectively. Share tips on maintaining positive relationships with their soon-to-be-former colleagues and how to prepare for the transition into their new role. Your support during this time can make all the difference in ensuring a smooth and confident transition. It's important for them to not feel alone in this process. You have built a great relationship with them; you are now courting them to their first day and beyond. Keep them close. When background checks or hiring processes take too long, it gives them pause and a chance to be recruited elsewhere. Let them know what to expect and keep them updated on the progress. I cannot express enough the importance of this!!!

Final Thoughts

You've done a great job in verbally securing an amazing candidate and starting the onboarding and courting process. However, as a recruiter, your job is not done. This stage starts to bleed into Stage 8 because you are moving to post-offer immediately after an offer is accepted.

Making a thoughtful and well-executed offer sets the stage for a strong start to the candidate's journey with the company. The clarity established in Stages 1–6 ensures that the offer aligns perfectly with the candidate's expectations and the company's needs. For instance, the groundwork laid in defining role requirements and pre-qualifying candidates helps eliminate uncertainties, making the offer stage more efficient and impactful. By addressing all aspects—who delivers the offer, the next steps, and clear expectations, ensure a smooth transition into onboarding. Remember, the work you do here directly impacts retention and long-term success for both the candidate and the organization.

Let's continue building a successful journey for your new hire!

Stage 8 - Post-Offer

Stage 8 of the Talent Acquisition Life Cycle is the Post-Offer phase, where the focus is on ensuring a smooth transition for the candidate who has accepted the offer.

This stage involves several crucial steps to foster a positive experience for the new employee (not just three this time). 10 to be exact:

1. Welcome Call

The hiring manager or another representative should make a welcome call to the candidate. This call serves to congratulate them on the decision, provide a warm welcome, and set the tone for a positive start. During the call, consider sharing details about the team's excitement, a preview of the onboarding process, or a personal message from the hiring manager about why they're thrilled to have the candidate on board. These elements can make the candidate feel valued and reassured in their decision.

This can be done once the offer letter is signed. AND yes, it really should be a call. This is NOT the same as the email congratulating them on the verbal offer. If this call needs to be scheduled, the recruiter should set it up for the hiring manager. Candidates have lots of options; you have to keep them close!

2. Paperwork and Onboarding Details

Clearly communicate to the candidate what paperwork or documentation they need to complete before their start date. Ensure they are well-informed about the onboarding process, including any forms, policies, or procedures they need to be aware of. I recommend providing candidates with a detailed checklist with clear timelines to alleviate their anxiety about starting a new role, allowing them to focus on preparing mentally and emotionally for their first day. You will need to coordinate heavily with HR. You must be on the same page!

3. Introduction to Peers

Ask the hiring manager to please consider introducing the candidate to a peer or peers in advance of their start date. These introductions can significantly ease the candidate's anxieties by providing a sense of familiarity and connection before their first day. Establishing early relationships helps candidates feel welcomed and integrated into the team, creating a positive foundation for their new role. This initial connection can help ease any anxieties and provide a friendly face on the first day. Maybe someone who was part of the interview process, or maybe someone brand new. The hiring manager can make this introduction by email or LinkedIn.

4. Coaching on Giving Notice

Transitioning from one job to another can be stressful. The recruiter should offer coaching on how to give notice to their current employer. Advise them to keep it short, express gratitude, and emphasize what they've learned in their current role.

Ask them to call or text you immediately so you are aware it's done. Congratulate them again; this is a hard process, and they are no doubt feeling relieved.

5. Follow-Up and Support

Encourage the candidate to reach out and share how the notice period is going. This can also be a tough-to-navigate time. Keep an open line of communication, showing support and addressing any concerns they might have during this transition period.

6. Regular Check-Ins

Schedule regular check-ins every three to four days before the start date. Change the check-ins between texts, emails, and phone calls. During these check-ins, discuss any updates regarding the onboarding process, answer questions about their new role, and address any concerns they may have.

Share progress on preparations for their arrival, such as team introductions or equipment setup, and remind them of what to expect on their first day to keep their excitement and engagement high. Inquire about their feelings and any needs they might have and reassure them that you are there to support them throughout the process. Share with them the onboarding and training preparation the department is doing for them and make them feel part of the team and excited about getting started!

7. First Day Preparation

Provide essential information for the candidate's first day, including:

- Arrival time.
- Contact person.
- Building and suite access details.
- Parking information.
- Lunch arrangements.

8. Equipment and System Setup

Ensure the candidate's workspace is fully set up on the first day. Having the necessary equipment, access to systems, and a designated go-to person demonstrates preparedness and professionalism. While this may be out of the recruiter's hands, it's important that you coordinate with the team that manages this so that you know they are prepared for your candidate to come in.

9. Positive Reinforcement

Use this time to reaffirm the candidate that they have made a great decision. Emphasize the exciting journey ahead and express confidence in their success within the organization. Continue to encourage team members or hiring managers to keep in touch with the candidate.

10. Candidate Experience Focus

Remember that even though the candidate has accepted the offer, they are still in the transition phase. Positive candidate experience remains crucial, and the support provided during this stage contributes significantly to their overall impression of the company.

By meticulously managing the post-offer phase, organizations can reinforce a positive candidate experience, set the stage for successful onboarding, and contribute to the new employee's sense of belonging and confidence in their decision. The clarity and groundwork laid in Stages 1–7—such as defining requirements, prequalifying candidates, and managing offers—play a critical role in ensuring a seamless and impactful transition into Stage 8.

Final Thoughts

The candidate experience now becomes the employee experience. To ensure long-term satisfaction and retention, focus on creating a seamless onboarding process that reinforces the trust and excitement built during the hiring stages. Regular communication, clear expectations, and continued engagement with both the candidate and their team can significantly enhance their sense of belonging and commitment to the organization.

This is so important in a world where candidates and employees have choices. By staying engaged and supportive, you're setting the stage for retention and long-term success.

Onto Stage 9! Let's go!

Stage 9 - Post-Hire

Stage 9 of the TA Life Cycle is the Post-Hire phase, where the recruiter's role extends beyond the candidate's first day of work.

This stage focuses on maintaining and building relationships with the new employee, ensuring their smooth integration into the company, and gathering valuable feedback for continuous improvement.

Here's a breakdown of 10 key actions and considerations for the recruiter to take in the Post-Hire stage:

1. Follow-up within the First 10-15 Days

Initiate a follow-up with the new employee shortly after they start their role. The goal is to assess their experience, address any concerns, and gather feedback that can be shared with the hiring manager and/or HR. During this conversation, consider asking questions like, 'How was your onboarding experience?' or 'Is there anything you need to feel more supported in your role?' These specific prompts can provide actionable insights and help reinforce their confidence in joining the company. Use this opportunity to check if they feel aligned with their role and to reinforce their decision to join the company.

2. Ask for Referrals

Leverage the positive relationship built with the new employee to request referrals. Happy employees are often more willing to share their connections and provide valuable leads for future hires. Frame this request as an opportunity to bring great talent to their team and strengthen their work environment.

3. Feedback Loop with Hiring Manager

Engage in a feedback session with the hiring manager to evaluate the overall hiring process. Discuss specific metrics such as time-to-hire, candidate quality, and retention rates. Additionally, explore questions like, 'Were there any stages that felt rushed or unnecessary?' or 'What aspects of the process should be emphasized more in future hires?' to ensure actionable outcomes. Identify what worked well and areas that could be improved in the future. This information is invaluable for streamlining processes and enhancing efficiency in future hires.

4. Continuous Learning

Use the post-hire stage as an opportunity for continuous learning. Reflect on the recruitment process, identify successes and challenges, and incorporate these insights into refining recruitment strategies and your entire process. Encourage team discussions to share these lessons and foster collective growth.

5. Knowledge Sharing

Share insights gained from post-hire interactions with the wider recruitment team and relevant stakeholders. Knowledge sharing contributes to collective learning and improvement. For example, noting trends in candidate satisfaction can guide process enhancements.

6. Check-In Periodically

Continue to stay connected with the new employee in the initial months, ideally every couple of months during the first year. These regular check-ins allow you to identify potential retention risks early, such as misaligned expectations or integration challenges, and address them proactively to ensure the employee feels supported and valued.

Regular check-ins help gauge job satisfaction, ensure alignment with expectations, and address any emerging issues. For example, a simple conversation about their progress or challenges can provide insights that are invaluable to the hiring manager.

7. Long-Term Relationship Building

Maintain a long-term relationship with the candidate,

extending beyond the initial year. Periodic check-ins, even if less frequent, demonstrate ongoing interest and support. This fosters loyalty and ensures that employees feel valued beyond their hiring phase.

8. Relationship Maintenance

Recognize that the relationship with the candidate doesn't end when they become an employee. Ongoing support could include periodic check-ins to discuss career progression, sharing relevant training or development opportunities, or inviting them to participate in company events. These engagement activities not only help maintain a positive connection but also demonstrate a genuine commitment to their growth and satisfaction. Exceptional recruiters are adept at maintaining connections and fostering positive relationships throughout the candidate's tenure. This connection can lead to long-term opportunities, such as internal promotions or future referrals.

9. Calendar Reminders

Schedule calendar reminders for follow-up check-ins. This ensures that these interactions are not overlooked and remain a consistent part of the recruiter's ongoing responsibilities. Automation tools can help streamline this process and maintain consistency.

10. Adaptation for Future Hires

Apply the feedback and lessons learned to adapt and enhance strategies for future hires in similar roles or departments. Tailoring strategies based on past experience ensures a continually improving recruitment process.

Final Thoughts

By actively participating in the post-hire phase, recruiters contribute to the overall success of the talent acquisition process. These efforts lead to improved employee retention, enhanced employer branding, and a more engaged workforce, showcasing the recruiter's impact on long-term organizational success. Continuous communication, relationship building, and feedback collection enable recruiters to refine their approaches and deliver exceptional value to both candidates and hiring managers. In the world of talent acquisition, the journey doesn't end; it transforms into a cycle of learning, improvement, and relationship building. The transition from candidate to employee is a critical moment to reinforce satisfaction and retention, ensuring long-term success.

Panna knows, and now, so do you!

Closing

We've finally reached the end of this journey, and what a journey it's been! There is so much more that I haven't covered in this book than I cover in live training and coaching sessions. That includes worksheets, homework, and other nuggets.

Recruiting isn't rocket science, but it's also not easy if you are doing it right. Doing it right means committing to a structured process, staying intentional in your actions, and prioritizing quality over speed. It's about truly understanding the needs of both the candidate and the hiring manager, building relationships, and ensuring every hire aligns with long-term success. If you are not passionate about making strong matches, uncovering top talent, and recruiting with intention and integrity, you are in the wrong field.

We get a bad rap as recruiters. I've always said,

"Recruiting is a dirty word." This reputation often stems from experiences with recruiters who prioritize quantity over quality or fail to follow up effectively, leaving candidates and companies feeling undervalued and underwhelmed. The methods outlined in this book aim to address these challenges by emphasizing intentionality, relationship-building, and a structured approach that ensures every interaction is meaningful and impactful. When someone asks you what you do and you say recruiting, many times, the conversation dies down quickly due to assumptions, or even worse, the person disengages.

Be the change. Call people back. Follow up. Do the right things.

And yes, candidates and hiring managers treat us the same way at times, but to make any change, we need to work on making a difference in ourselves. Lead the way.

Take pride in your work. Hire a coach to support you outside of your organization. Hire me.
I train individuals and teams in this process, and I

coach individuals as well at all levels. I strictly focus on TA/Recruiting, sticking to what I know. Although I am the CEO of PKR, I am a passionate recruiter at heart, and I am glad I am able to share all this wisdom with you.

This entire process is built on the philosophy that recruiting is not just about filling positions; it's about creating intentional, meaningful matches that benefit both the candidate and the organization. For example, in Stage 4, the focus on prequalification ensures that candidates align with both the role and the company culture, while Stage 6's emphasis on decision-making solidifies the match through clear evaluation criteria and feedback loops.

By integrating these structured stages, the process becomes a roadmap for achieving impactful and lasting connections. By following a structured process, you ensure consistency, integrity, and quality in every step.

I hope we have an opportunity to meet. Thank you for reading my book. Use it as a workbook. Take notes, highlight, earmark, reference it with each candidate, and search.

Happy hiring!
-K

About the Author

For Kelly Robinson, recruiting is a *dirty* word. It's been tarnished by outdated processes, impersonal interactions, lack of interaction at all, and a relentless focus on speed over quality. But Kelly is on a mission to change that—to take the *dirty* out of recruiting and transform it into a structured, intentional, and successful process that benefits both companies and candidates.

As the powerhouse behind *Next Level Recruiting* and the *9 Stages of the Talent Acquisition Life Cycle*, Kelly has spent over two decades redefining how organizations attract, hire, and retain top talent. With a sharp eye for strategy and an unwavering commitment to hiring with intention, she's helped over 500 companies bring in more than 15,000 candidates—transforming careers and businesses along the way.

But Kelly's journey isn't just about business success—it's about resilience, reinvention, and the power of betting on yourself. After dedicating 13 years to an executive role, she received a life-changing phone call: she was out. Fired. No warning, no cushion. Instead of dwelling on the setback, she turned it into her launching pad. Two days later, she founded PKRecruiting (PKR), built it from the ground up, and by 2020, it had already hit seven figures. Not just a financial milestone, but proof that when you know your worth, you don't wait for permission to succeed.

Beyond recruiting, Kelly is a single mom raising an incredible son, Erik, who keeps her grounded, inspired, and endlessly entertained with his hockey skills and sharp mind. She's a Philly sports fanatic (GO Birds!), a devoted dog mom to two Cavapoos, and someone who thrives on structure but still embraces life's unpredictability. Whether she's traveling to sunny vacation spots, advising and training talent acquisition professionals on her *Next Level Recruiting* framework, or leading her team to success on supporting client recruitment projects, Kelly is always in motion—always pushing forward.

Through *Next Level Recruiting*, she's giving HR pros and talent acquisition professionals at all levels the playbook to hire with precision, lead with confidence, and create workplaces where people *want* to stay. Because for Kelly, recruiting isn't just business—it's personal.

Efficiency

Kelly attributes her remarkable achievements to her ability to balance entrepreneurship with single motherhood. Juggling the responsibilities of parenthood and business, she has mastered the art of efficiency, ensuring that every moment counts. This ethos extends into PKR's operations, where her focus on building relationships and providing top-tier recruitment, training, and coaching services has become the cornerstone of her success. For Kelly, it's not just about making hires; it's about creating operational excellence that translates into seamless candidate experiences.

Client-Centric Approach

PKR is a comprehensive recruitment services firm

specializing in tailored solutions for companies of all sizes. For example, PKR has successfully partnered with fast-growing startups to design end-to-end recruitment processes that scale with their rapid growth. From strategic talent acquisition consulting to hands-on recruiting, PKR offers a suite of services designed to meet diverse hiring needs. These include outsourced recruitment (all or partial), interim recruiting, recruiting support, emerging recruitment leadership coaching, and the Next Level Recruiting training program for recruiters. PKR's hallmark is its focus on building long-term partnerships with clients, ensuring every hiring decision aligns with their unique business goals and culture.

Most of PKR's clients are not just one-time collaborators but repeat partners, many of whom have worked with Kelly in the past or come through referrals. This trust underscores her commitment to delivering results and fostering meaningful relationships.

Operational Excellence

Operational excellence is not just a phrase for Kelly; it's a philosophy. For instance, one of PKR's long-term clients, a rapidly growing tech startup, faced challenges with high turnover and misaligned hires. Kelly implemented a data-driven recruiting strategy, streamlined the interview process, and introduced comprehensive onboarding practices. As a result, the client saw a 40% increase in employee retention within the first year, proving that operational excellence translates directly into measurable success. From candidate sourcing to post-hire follow-ups, every facet of PKR's approach is designed to deliver quality service that transcends expectations. Her focus on consistency and intentionality ensures that both candidates and clients benefit from a process that is as thoughtful as it is effective.

Recognized Thought Leader

Kelly is a recognized thought leader in the talent acquisition space, with 35,000+ followers on LinkedIn, and is frequently sought after for her insights on recruitment trends, leadership, organizational growth, AI-powered hiring, pay transparency, and more. She has been featured in numerous prominent publications and platforms, including **Fast Company**, where she discussed the impact of AI on hiring, and **Forage**, where she shared strategies for effective communication in remote work. Additionally, her thought leadership has been highlighted in **International Business Times**, **HR Daily Advisor**, **Ph.Creative**, **HR.com**, **Home Business Magazine**, **International Business Times**, **Unleash**, **TestGorilla Blog**, **TechBullion**, **Success Magazine**, **Audacity.com**, **Ms. Career Girl**, and more.

Balancing Act

Balancing her professional achievements with personal responsibilities, Kelly is a proud single mother to her son Erik, a high school athlete with aspirations as big as his mom's. Her personal experiences have shaped her empathetic and empowering leadership style, making her a sought-after speaker, coach, and mentor in the talent acquisition space.

Passion and Purpose

Kelly's passion extends beyond business. She's an advocate for intentionality in work and life, inspiring others to lead with purpose, authenticity, and heart. Through her book, training programs, and coaching initiatives, Kelly empowers recruiters and leaders to rethink traditional models, embrace innovation, and foster meaningful connections that drive success for years to come.

In "Next Level Recruiting," Kelly distills her wealth of experience into a roadmap for recruiters worldwide, providing actionable insights to navigate the ever-changing landscape of talent acquisition. Her story is not just one of professional triumph but a testament to what's possible when passion, efficiency, and commitment converge. Let her journey inspire you to embrace innovation, prioritize meaningful connections, and redefine what success looks like in your own life and career.

Kelly Robinson

www.ingramcontent.com/pod-product-compliance
Lightning Source LLC
Chambersburg PA
CBHW070943210326
41520CB00021B/7024